PAIN, TEARS, AND TESTIMONY

From the loss of a Mother to
reuniting with my Father

ALBERT BENEDICT CASSELL JR.

WESTBOW
PRESS®
A DIVISION OF THOMAS NELSON
& ZONDERVAN

WestBow Press books may be ordered through booksellers or by contacting:

WestBow Press
A Division of Thomas Nelson & Zondervan
1663 Liberty Drive
Bloomington, IN 47403
www.westbowpress.com
844-714-3454

ISBN: 978-1-6642-7640-6 (sc)
ISBN: 978-1-6642-7642-0 (hc)
ISBN: 978-1-6642-7641-3 (e)

Library of Congress Control Number: 2022915958

Print information available on the last page.

WestBow Press rev. date: 1/31/2023

Commit to the Lord whatever you do,
and he will establish your plans.
Proverbs 16:3 (NIV)

Dedication

No one can tell your story better than you can. This book is dedicated to my wife Crystal G. Cassell, to my sons, Khalil, Alijah, Asaiah, and Azaniah. Your love and your patience, has allowed me time to grow into what God has called me to be.

SPECIAL THANKS

Special thanks to my father Albert Benedict Cassell Sr. and mother Sophie Muhlenburg Cassell (deceased), who made the sacrifice to travel to the United States to make a better life for their family. To my siblings, Prince, Sylvia, Vera, Steven, Darryl, Albertine, and Sophie, words could not express my appreciation and love for you.

To my father and mother in-law, Kevin and Maryann Mathews, thank you. To my nieces, nephews, extended family, friends, etc., thank you.

To Andrew Huang and the whole team from MTV, I would not be where I am today without you. You changed my life, thank you. To Prince William County, VA, the entire fire service, all public servants, Milton Hershey School, Winston-Salem State University, Prov-City, you all have played a significant part in my journey, thank you.

To my shepherd, Rev. Dr. Joshua Speights Jr., and the Neabsco Baptist Church family, the body of Christ, thank you for your mentorship, your prayers and your unconditional love for me and my family.

Al

PREFACE

"Influential I am at that, couldn't be a hustler, couldn't carry the strap, Aye yo, I pray for my homies, like my cousin J Mack, who was riding for his sister and took a shank to the back. How real is this, or how real is that, on my way to college, flushed an eight ball of crack."

"4 Candles"
Biga Boys Club

No one, including myself, knew just how serious my alcohol problem had become. I moved home to Rhode Island when my mother died after her battle with brain cancer. My intention was to move home and assist with the care of my twelve-year-old sister and younger brother Darryl. My older sister Vera was already doing her best to hold down the home at 226 Vermont Avenue while still trying to maintain her own family. I knew I had to do something, my intentions were good, but when God is in the rearview and not leading, it is very easy to get engulfed in the trap of the enemy. To be all the way honest with you, I got caught up. I could not deal with the pain that came with my mother's illness and untimely loss. The struggle was real. I saw a strong, bold, and vibrant woman just dwindle away to cancer. She never gave up, and she fought the good fight until her very last breath. She was a true soldier for Christ, still giving God the praise while enduring sickness and affliction. There were many days when I could see that her concern was for the well-being of her children and what was going to happen to them when she was gone.

You never know how you are going to react to a real situation until a real situation happens. The day before my mother died, I was in New York City working. My younger brother called me. "What's going on, bro?" He told me in so many words that I needed to come home. Disturbed by this revelation, I first went to the corner store to purchase twenty-two ounces of cold beer. This was my way of coping when things became overwhelming. I came back to the production studio I was working in and turned that bottle up 90 degrees. I finished my assignment, and told my supervisor that I had to go home.

I called my girlfriend at the time and explained to her what was going on. I told her I needed to get to Rhode Island right away. I wanted her to be by my side but really did not know how to express that. At the time I was so agitated and fearful of the unknown. I raced down to the Port Authority bus terminal and got on the first bus going to Providence, Rhode Island. When I touched down, I walked in the front door and immediately felt that weight hit me. This would be the weight I would carry for years to come. I went straight upstairs to see mommy. My gut told me something was different—I could feel it. I laid down in front of her door that night and waited to see what the morning would bring. *Lord, do something*, I prayed silently. *I do not know if I am ready for what is happening right now.*

The next morning, the hospice nurses and attendants came to the house. On this particular morning, we also had a grief counselor coming to speak to the family. I still remember my dad calling everyone to the living room for our family meeting. The counselor approached us with a humble spirit and tried in her best way to explain the transition process, in preparing for our mother to die. All I could think about was, *What are you talking about? Mommy is going to be good. She is a soldier, throughout her illness when things seemed to get bad, there was always another surgery, another treatment, but now you're telling me this is it, the end? Sophie Muhlenburg Cassell? No way. I don't believe it, I won't accept it, no.*

Before the counselor could finish talking, the attendant who was taking care of my mother walked slowly down the stairs in tears. She looked at all of us and said with great heaviness, "She's gone."

I sprinted up the stairs in disbelief, entering the room only to see mommy's lifeless body lying there as if she was just resting. I was stunned. I just sat there and stared for a million miles. *Is this really how it is going to end?*

PART ONE

FINDING MY FAITH

1

CHAPTER

ALBERT

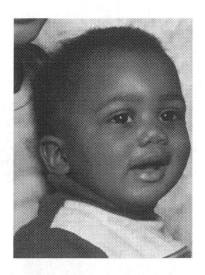

My name is Albert Benedict Cassell Jr., and I was born May 8, 1979, in Providence, Rhode Island. My parents immigrated from Liberia, West Africa. Being raised in an African culture in America was very humbling. I would not trade it for anything. It gave me a tough skin and the ability to adapt to adversity. My parents went through a lot to get to America for the purpose of making a better life for their family. They were young when they left Liberia in the late 1960s and early 1970s. Their first stop in America was New York City. Eventually, there were several family members and friends who would make that same journey. They came to America in search of streets of gold, but instead they got Harlem. Together, they did what they could to survive, working odd jobs in the garment district and piling up in small apartments to cut down living expenses. Eventually my parents decided to leave the city and move further north to Rhode Island. They were in search of new opportunities and a brighter future for their children.

We grew up in the West End neighborhood of Wiggins Village, where we lived in a three-bedroom town house on Dodge Street. There were always people coming in and out of the house because my parents loved big. If family or friends were visiting or just coming to the United States for the first time, our home was the transition point.

Prince, Albert, Vera, Mommy

Sylvia, Albert, and Vera

My family seemed to grow by the week, but our core team was my older brother Prince, my older cousin Sylvia, my sister Vera, and myself. My siblings and I would often get picked on in the neighborhood and at school because of our African culture. There was no internet at the time so all people generally knew about Africa was what they heard or seen on some commercial showing poverty, and illness. There was a general assumption that all Africans lived in huts and smelled bad. And to be truthful, we assumed the worst of our new neighbors as well. There were many fights, and tension growing up in my neighborhood. My older brother, while playing basketball one day, got into an altercation that resulted in him having to go to the hospital. We were constantly harassed with phases like "African bush booger" and anything else that could provoke a fight. There were some wins, some losses, but God!

This was all growing pains, but these incidents can cause internal conflict and trauma if not dealt with in a healthy way. We were raised to show no emotion, to be strong, "be a man." If someone hit you, you hit them back harder. When we don't deal with our internal trauma, it manifests in ways that we did not expect. True conflict resolution is key and needs to be modeled for children. Not everything has to be zero to one hundred. Not every conflict means war. There are other options if you take the time to listen to that small, still voice.

I was picked on for being African, dark-skinned, and overweight. When kids found out that my name was Albert, most of the time the next thing to come out of their mouths was "Hey, hey, hey, it's Fat Albert." Kids had a unique way of motivating you back then, and while it wasn't right, I dished out my fair share as well. This is what we knew then, but we know better now, and therefore we must strive to do better.

I too hurt others, I too was the bully, please forgive me for my ignorance, and my frustrations while navigating my own existence. Forgiveness is key, but most importantly, I forgive me.

Growing up in our home, there was lots of laughter and love. Prince was the star basketball player, Sylvia had all the latest music on vinyl, and my parents were raising this family in the hood. My sister Vera and I were the closest in age. On the weekend, I would go find my cousin Ricky, who lived two courts over from us. Our weekends were full of adventure. One day we decided to take a ride up Broad Street to Oakland Cemetery to put flowers on my cousin Simeon's grave. He was young when he died, and it devastated us all. I still remember it like it was yesterday. He was at our house, playing and wrestling with us, and when it was time to leave that day, he would not stop waving. As I look back on it now, it seemed as if he was telling us goodbye for the last time.

When our cousin died, it was the first time any of us had ever experienced death with someone that close to us. Simeon, Ricky, and Vera were all the same age and were the first of our generation to be born in the United States. Simeon was a special needs child who was full of love and full of life. We all knew that he was different, but that did not change our love or make any difference to the way that we treated him.

The death of Simeon caused me to reflect on my young life. It was the first time I thought about the uncertainty of the future and what was truly out there. Love you always, until we meet again cousin.

Make your kisses count. Life is precious and not something you ever want to take for granted. You can be here today and gone tomorrow. Make every second and every breath be with great purpose. Your kisses count when those receiving can kiss back. Give your flowers while your loved ones can still smell them.

That said, I grew up a bit paranoid because it seemed there was always someone around me having some sort of near-death experience. It was common language in the family. The conversation would usually start off with something like, "You boy, I almost died last night, you hear me?" I never could understand why they would even go there.

When Vera was younger and had gone away to camp, someone pushed her into a pool. She could not swim. The lifeguard jumped in and was able to save her. She doesn't seem to remember this story so I don't know where I got that from? A similar situation happened to me at Bucklin Pool in Providence, but my sister was quick to react and caught me. One day years later, my sister was choking in our living room, and I had to act quickly to perform the Heimlich maneuver. After a few thrusts, out came a piece of plastic that she had been chewing on.

God is amazing: we are even now, no more! I'm speaking and declaring life over everything around me. Looking back, I can see the battle beginning to take place. The enemy was trying to get us out of here early, but God is faithful and encamps his angels around the righteous—not because of our works but because of his integrity.

> For we wrestle not against flesh and blood, but against principalities, against powers, against the rulers of the darkness of this world, against spiritual wickedness in high places. (Ephesians 6:12 KJV)

Spiritual warfare was something we were introduced to very early in my life. Not because it was something that we were looking for—it just kind of came by default. It wasn't until many years later that I would have a better understanding of what all of this meant in regards to the calling on my life. As kids, we would wake up in the middle of the night to see Mommy praying. When I went off to boarding school for the first time, Mommy made sure that she sent me with my Bible and a bottle of holy oil. I did not understand it then, but I realize now that the battle we face is unseen. The only way to fight a spiritual battle is with the spirit of God.

Every battle is unique, so it is best always to stay in some mode of preparation. When Mommy died, my life came to a stretching halt. I left my job as an associate producer at MTV Networks to move back to Rhode Island. The objective was to help raise my younger sister. At the time, my father was transitioning back to Africa, a dream he and my mother had shared for as long as I could remember. We all agreed that it would be best for my sister to stay in America initially until he was able to get things settled.

I did not realize how much the illness and death of my mother had taken a toll on my father. I saw things from the outside looking in, not realizing the true impact. We all grieve in different ways. My father had lost someone he had known a majority of his life, the loss was big for us all, but I could not relate to what he could have been going through. I can truly say that I have a greater love and appreciation for my father since becoming a father and a husband. Through it all, he fulfilled his vows for better or worse, through sickness and health. Until her last breath, he was there. The Bible tells us that love conquers a multitude of sins, and this is the promise that we stand on. Dad, I salute you, I honor you, I love you.

Albert Sr. and Albert Jr.

2

CHAPTER

THE HAT

My decision to move back home to Rhode Island was not an easy one. I had allot going for me in New York. Things were great at MTV: I was traveling, making money, and working on some reputable projects. I am so grateful and blessed to have received such an opportunity of a lifetime.

Andrew Huang changed my life when he came to small hole-in-the-wall club in North Carolina and offered me an internship that would launch me into my first career. I first met Andrew when he and his MTV crew came to Winston-Salem State University's homecoming to film the Jay-Z episode of *Diary*. I was a junior in college and was fresh off line. For those not familiar with this term, "off line" is when you complete the process of joining a fraternity. My main focus when I arrived at WSSU was to join, and once that was accomplished, I did not know what else to do with myself. My brother Miko introduced me to a promotion company called Off the Hook entertainment. I was not sure what I was getting into, but it turned out to be a major move and blessing all at the same time. I am so grateful for the men who helped to orchestrate and provide this opportunity. JG, G, Bam, Gary, etc, Thank you.

On that particular October night, I really did not know what I was supposed to be doing in my new role. One thing I did know, I had to be fresh. Off the Hook was hosting the official after party for Roc-A-Fella Records artist Jay-Z at Club 2000. For hours I contemplated which outfit, shoes, and accessories to wear. I finally broke down and asked Miko if I should top the outfit off and wear my orange derby hat to match the shirt and slacks. "Bro, am I doing too much if I wear the hat?" Miko convinced me that the hat was a go. That was all I needed to hear—it was show time.

We felt like we were the celebrities pulling up at the club that night.

It was a sight to see that many people jam-packed in a club to see their favorite rapper. That night I posted up in the VIP area where Jay-Z and his entourage would be once they entered the club. It was hot. It felt like a heat wave and I could feel the beads of sweat dancing on my forehead. It was at that moment that I thought to myself that maybe I was overdressed for the occasion. This internal conflict continued as stood my post but I was convinced I had made the right decision. Down South, in a potentially hostile environment, you don't want to be mistaken for something you are not. I was there to do a job. I took my assignment that night too serious—I felt like I just received word that I would be protecting the president of the United States of America.

As the anticipation grew, the crowd in the club became restless. Suddenly black vehicles pulled up, and as the doors opened, Jay and his crew got out and entered the club. The scene erupted. Jay-Z, entourage, and camera crew were quickly escorted to the VIP area where I stood post. I felt like I had a purpose now. I did not care if all the people in the club laughed at my hat, outfit, and said, "Man. I know you are hot." I kept a straight face but continued to wipe the sweat from my forehead.

I could tell immediately that this was not the most comfortable environment for Jay-Z. The more people jammed their way into the club, the more it became uncomfortable for all. While Jay-Z and his entourage were attempting to mingle within the crowd, the energy in the club shifted. Shortly thereafter a drink was thrown on one of the recording artists who accompanied Jay-Z that night. As the artist quickly took off into the crowd, Jay-Z went after him. Again, the club erupted. I instantly went after Jay, his entourage, and the camera crew to make sure that they got back to the VIP area safely. There was some pushing and shoving as we cleared a path for them to get out of the general area of the club. By the time they got back to the VIP area, they all had decided it was time to leave.

Before they left, I spoke with one of the camera crew members, Andrew, who was very grateful that I was able to help clear a way for him to get his camera shots. I did not realize I was doing this at the time—I was just acting out of instinct. He then asked me if there was anything he could do for me.

I replied, "An internship." That was the first thing that came to mind without even putting much thought into it.

Andrew handed me a business card and instructed me to send him an email with my résumé. The rest is history. It was a moment that literally changed my life. When the Diary of Jay-Z finally aired, what stood out the most from the shoving in the club scene was my orange derby hat. Thank you Miko.

I went on to intern at MTV that summer and eventually transitioned to a full-time position with the network after I completed college. Andrew, Jason, Vinny, Scottie, Mike, Ev, Elis, and so many more showed me everything that I needed to know about TV production and News documentaries. Words could not even come close to expressing my gratitude and love. I have learned that preparation is everything. It's about not only being in the right place at the right time but being prepared for the blessing when it lands on your doorstep.

3
CHAPTER

WELCOME TO MARS

When my mother died, the decision to leave NYC was extremely difficult to make. At the time, I felt it was only right to move home to help take care of the family. Maybe some of it was my emotions taking over, but God ultimately had his hand in all of it. I did not realize I was the one in need of help. I fell into a deep depression and suppressed it with alcohol, chain-smoking, and enjoying the everyday pleasures of life. I was in self-destruct mode, hoping that it might get me closer to seeing Mommy again.

To make things worse, I could not find a job in my field. I was filled with pride and arrogance; I often turned down positions because they were not going to pay me what I felt I was worth. I had to take on this attitude living in the city because it was the only way to survive. Eventually reality began to sit in and the bills began to pile up. I became desperate for work. I turned to the temp agency Labor Ready, which hired day workers for hard manual labor. You have to be up early in the morning to sign in at the office, where you will find plastic lawn chairs and stale coffee. You wait for them to call your name and give you a work ticket. Talk about a piece of humble pie! Not too long ago I'm at the Video Music Awards and now I'm forced to take labor positions to keep the lights on. If I was blessed to get work that particular day, I would bring home somewhere between thirty to sixty dollars—and half of that was going to alcohol, which only fed a deeper depression. *Wow, has it really come to this?* I found myself wondering. *Welcome home, guy, welcome home.*

I knew that the only way to break out of this depression was to tap into my creative energy. I got my HD camera and began to film around the city. What started off as general b-roll and interviews evolved in what became the *Prov-City We on Mars* DVD. The DVD was a success and exactly what the city had been waiting for. Ever since I first left Rhode Island in the eighth grade to attend boarding school in Pennsylvania, I had a desire to give back to my city. This was it. The DVD highlighted established and new talent from around the city. Prov-City We on Mars offered a positive platform for artists to express themselves. My goal was to show the city that we all have the same dreams, same struggles, and that it was important for us to work together while reaching beyond the concrete jungle that many of us were born into. Reaching for the stars, all the way to Mars. I would spend hours in the lab, editing to make sure there was no footage that could potentially provoke hate or violence. The goal was to create our own identity while coming together on the common ground of music and creativity. Prov City DVD will always be a unique piece of history for Providence. Thank you, I could not have done it without you, Prov City—We still on Mars.

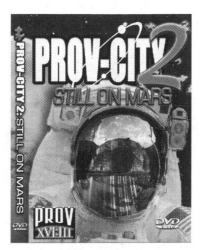

Prov City 2: Still on Mars

THE YARD

A year later, I met a beautiful young woman named Crystal on the campus of Brown University. Neither Crystal nor I attended the school. I was a graduate of Winston-Salem State University, and Crystal was attending Johnson & Wales University. At the time, I was somewhere between Mars and Zucolo. In other words, I was lost. The DVD was gaining traction, but not enough to support me financially. I was still depressed, binge drinking and many days were just a blur. I knew I was struggling but did not have the time or the resources to address it properly.

One bright Spring Day I decided to change up the scenery. My best friend Charles drove me over to the campus. Charles and I had 1st met as teenagers when were both were working for Shaw's supermarket. We both ended up going to college in North Carolina, spent time in NYC, and moved back to Rhode Island at the same time. Yes, that's my road dog, that's family. There was a cookout on Brown University's campus, and Charles and I showed up. As we arrived on campus, I was getting out of the vehicle when I saw Crystal walking towards me. She was beautiful, and for a moment time stood still. This is a feeling that you don't experience every day, when you do find this, stay awhile and let the moment marinate.

BIBLE ON THE DRESSER

Crystal and I kicked it off well. She was from Rhode Island but grew up in California. Her father served in the United States Marine Corp. and spent his career on the West Coast, raising his family. Crystal and I shared a love for hip-hop music, the water, Mexican food, and pain. Because of this common ground, things began to progress quickly between us. I felt good to be able to escape from my current reality and just smile while getting fat. When we were together, we laughed, drank, and ate well. Nothing else in the world seemed to matter. Crystal was special, a single mother raising a four-year-old, working a full-time job, and finishing up her finance degree.

On many evenings, we would dream together. We shared our passions in life and talked about our future while moonlighting in the backyard. One evening while visiting Crystal at her home, I noticed a Bible on her dresser. I asked her if I could read it, and she agreed. It was the New International Version (NIV), which was easier for me to read, compared to the King James Version. I grew up in the Baptist Church for most of my life, but like many I drifted from a place of being authentic to my faith. This Bible was staring me right in my face, telling me to stop running. Occasionally I would take in a few words of uplift and insight. It was the first time in a long time that I was actually able to read scripture and retain it—a great feeling.

Crystal and I dated for a while but broke it off after a few months. After being in this place of euphoria, everything between us came to a screeching halt. For me, things seemed to be too much, too fast, and too soon. There was some drama with exes, and I was still trying to wrap my head around the responsibility that came with dating a single mother. In the past, I would run when things became uncomfortable for me, so this is what I defaulted to.

Shortly after we separated, Crystal dropped off an NIV Bible with my name engraved on it in gold. It was a nice gift, but I was not in the right headspace. I would have felt really bad throwing away a Bible, because you just don't do that. So, I shelved it.

The next year was an emotional roller coaster. Through several ups and downs in both our lives, the Lord saw fit to bring us back together. We both had many close calls in our lives, and we knew that it was by God's grace we were spared. We began to see God's power manifest literally right in front of us. Through prayer and revelation, we both decided that we needed a real change. Renewing our faith in Jesus Christ was the plan, but we weren't really sure how to go about it. We did know that God preserved us for a reason. Our backgrounds and cultures were different but at the same time we had a lot in common. We began attending church, and while we were focused on him, the Lord meticulously began to order our steps.

Despite our concerted efforts, we fell short many times. It was around this time that we found out we were pregnant with our first child. God's Word holds true when it says that we all fall short of his glory. But if you make a mistake in life or you encounter a setback, don't give up—reset, and start again. Satan's job is to make you believe that it is over and you should just serve him. This is a lie straight from the pits of hell, and I'm speaking from experience. His job is to take you to hell, but that is his destiny, not yours.

FIGHT OR FLIGHT?

My relationship with my soon-to-be wife was a big deal for me. I knew at this point it was going to be fight or flight. Our culture has become too comfortable making babies with no follow through. This is not to say that just because your girlfriend is pregnant, you should get married. However, it shouldn't be off the table. Knowing the difference between love and lust will change your life. I operated in lust for most of my adulthood up until that point and because of this I ruined good friendships. Having the discernment to know why someone is in your life is truly a gift from God.

Crystal was already adulting; I was still a boy in a man's body. There was extra stress on me because I had to do my best not to be "that guy," but this was bad motivation. Comparing yourself to other people usually does not work out well: "what's for Jacob is not for John." We all have our own path. Ask God for his guidance and let the Spirit lead.

> If any of you lacks wisdom, you should ask God, who gives generously to all without finding fault, and it will be given to you. (James 1:5 NIV)

I knew that seeking counsel would be the wise thing to do. My uncle was a pastor, and I knew he would be a great resource. He recommended that we do Bible study sessions with him. It seemed a little strange, because we both were expecting him to recommend marriage or something along this line. We met for Bible study once a week and started in the Gospel of John. The more we engaged and learned from Bible study, the more the Word of God began to jump off the pages and into our life. From the outside, all the odds were against us. I did not have a stable job, 226, my parent's home I was living in was at risk of foreclosure, and my life at the time was a mess.

Crystal and I both decided that we needed a fresh start to get away from everything that was weighing us down in our hometown. We wanted a new perspective. I was focused on securing a stable job for my family when I discovered that the fire department was hiring in Virginia. We knew this would be an excellent opportunity to begin our new life together. At the time, I was taking EMT classes at the Community College of Rhode Island in hopes of landing a better job in the city. Through this building block, the fire department became more of a reality. During the recession of 2008, Rhode Island had the second-highest unemployment rate in the nation, behind Detroit, Michigan. It was time to go.

Through consistent efforts and prayer, I was offered the opportunity to train with the fire department in Northern Virginia through a mentorship program. I was nervous because this was not a guaranteed position, but I was stepping out on faith. The morning I received the call, Crystal encouraged me to take advantage of the opportunity. "You better not be here by the time I get off of work," she said.

I had one shot to get this done, and if I missed it, the opportunity might not come around again. At the time, I owned a 1995 Mazda 626 that would break down every time it stopped at a red light. How was I supposed to make a seven-hour trip to Northern Virginia? I had little to no money, but while I trained, I could stay with a cousin who lived in Maryland. I packed my bag and started my journey on 95 South. I was nervous about stopping for fuel, in fear the car might break down at a rest stop. I prayed, and the Lord delivered me to my destination safely with no problems at all. This was 100 percent God. I was destined for this.

My cousin's apartment in Maryland would become fertile ground for what God was sowing in our lives. I am forever grateful for my cousin and how God used her to help birth something greater than my eyes could see. To the stars, to Mars, and back again, cousin. Only God, only God. Thank you.

That summer I trained hard with hopes of getting the job offer then moving Crystal and Khalil down to Virginia. In my mind, it was already done. I visualized it, I wrote it down, and I knew it would happen. Sometimes you must get to the point where you just surrender and let the Spirit of God lead. When you start to do things that you cannot explain and say things that clearly do not align with your normal thinking, this is God. When you find yourself in this place, stay awhile and let it marinate. At the pace Crystal and I were moving, we were clearly on a mission. Finding a decent job to provide for our son and new baby on the way was a necessity.

While training in Virginia that summer, I worked several odd jobs to maintain an income. During that time, Charles moved down from Rhode Island. This was a game changer. Charles was very good at finding work. One day he invited me to an interview for a job that he was applying for. Charles thought it would be a good idea if I came along to see if there were any open positions for me. Off of the strength, I attended. I literally just pulled something out of my bag that looked halfway decent and threw it on. It felt like one of those *Pursuit of Happiness* moments, like when Will Smith's character shows up for the job interview with paint on his shirt.

As God would have it, without any notification, I showed up for the interview. One week later I was offered a position with benefits.

> And my God will meet all your needs according to the
> riches and glory in Christ Jesus. (Philippians 4:19)

This was big news. I immediately called Crystal and shared what just happened.

It was Labor Day weekend when we made our big move to Virginia. It was not long before we found our church home and rededicated our lives back to the Lord. Virginia was a breath of fresh air. For the first time, I saw young thriving families, God fearing men and women living on purpose. Not to say Rhode Island did not have this, I just couldn't see it.

This was something I dreamed of, but didn't know actually existed. Our son, Alijah Zion-Sede Cassell, was born in October, and Crystal and I were married the following month in our pastor's office. Afterwards, we went to Friday's restaurant to celebrate—just us, Crystal, Khalil and Alijah, our new little family.

With all that had taken place that summer, I did not get offered the job with the fire department. Charles and I worked together at an alternative school for youth. It was not what I had planned for, but the Lord provided a stable income and benefits. I learned more from working with the youth than they were supposed to be learning from me. This experience humbled me as I continued to grow with the Lord and with my new family.

But God will send you when you are ready. One year later, the fire department offered me the opportunity to attend their training academy. My start date was July 26th, which also happens to be The Liberian Independence Day. Everything seemed to align just right.

Prince William County, VA

4
CHAPTER

NEW WAY OF LIFE

Shortly after we moved to Virginia, things began to pick up quickly. My son Asaiah Benedict Cassell was born just as we were still adapting to life in the fire department. My younger sister Sophie who moved to the west coast to live with my older brother, relocated from California to move in with us. By the spring, it was clear a decision to sell 226 Vermont was going to have to be made. It was a hard decision for all of us to make but I knew we needed closure. We all did our best to keep things going but we were unable to keep up. While I was excited about all the new opportunities I was experiencing in Virginia; I was hurt because I knew my family was still going through it in Rhode Island. One of the hardest people for me to leave was my cousin Deron, affectionately known as "Byngo," This was my cousin Sylvia's 1st son so he was like a brother. Deron was always by my side along with my younger brother Darryl. When we began to transition out of Rhode Island, Darryl was attending school at Virginia State University. Things were different for Deron because he battled sickle cell disease all of his life. I would see my cousin Sylvia go back and forth to the hospital caring for Deron while caring for her other children, Toyin and Sade. If it were not for the care team that Deron had since being an infant, I know he would have moved with us to Virginia. These were some of the hardest decisions I ever had to make in my life. It was a heart break; the day we signed the house over to the new owner, we gained nothing and was able to just break even. It was hurtful, because I remember the day that Mom and I pulled up and saw the house for the first time. It was my mother's dream to buy a home for our family. Letting go of that home felt like letting a piece of Mommy go.

But through all the pain, I knew it was time to move on. During the period of time when we all first moved to Virginia, we all lived under the same roof. We brought a whole new meaning to the term "full house," but not too far from what I knew growing up. As adults we emulate what we were exposed to without even realizing it. We were now the Virginia Cassells, living in close quarters and with different personalities. I thought, *This is going to be fun.* You must be self-aware, because if you are not, depression will teach you a lesson.

Journal entry:

Lord, I know that no matter what, you have brought me through another year. I am thankful, and I praise you for what you are doing. Lord, there has been spiritual warfare taking place in my family. I know that you are aware, but I am coming to you and asking for your help. There has been negativity revolving around this family. There has been talk and sickness that has been claimed. Lord, we rebuke it all in the name of Jesus.

Lord, you are an awesome God. When my wife speaks, I know that it is not her talking. I don't know what is invading my home. Lord, I will not stop giving you the glory. You are my rock, my guide, and my protector; whom or what shall I fear? Lord, you are my hope in the midst of all the dark shadows. Help me this day. In the mighty name of Jesus, I pray. Amen.

MISSING FLORIDA

> There is no one holy like the Lord; there is no one besides
> I; there is no Rock like our God. (1 Samuel 2:2)

Raising a young family can be a big challenge in and of itself. Then you add a new career, a new marriage, and your siblings and friends in the home, you are in for a treat. Crystal and I had moved from a small two-bedroom apartment to a three-level townhome to accommodate our growing family. This came on the heels of a fire station transfer that I requested. I was going from my slow shift work station to a busy day work station. I was now working Monday through Friday from 0600 to 1800 hours. Prior to that I was working one twenty-four-hour shift and then having forty-eight hours off, only working nine days out of the month. I made this change with little to no regard for how it would impact my wife or my family. I was new in this field of public safety, and I was eager to gain more experience. Time would eventually show that this came at a huge expense.

Crystal was not feeling this move at all, and our marriage went for a somersault. Shortly after arriving at the new fire station, I had to make a decision whether to attend a very important technical rescue training or to join my family in Disney World for a trip planned previously. Because I wanted to prove that I belonged, I put my career and my personal desires before my family. But all the accolades, merits, and honors in the world mean nothing at all when you walk into an empty home. Pay close attention to her heart, as it is fragile. Love her as you love yourself.

> Husbands, love your wives, just as Christ loved the church
> and gave himself up for her
> (Ephesians 5:25)

A LETTER TO CRYSTAL

Good afternoon, Crystal.

Regarding the conflict that we have with my scheduled training and vacation, I don't want this to hinder us once again. We have been making progress, and the only way to go at this point, is forward. I am thankful for the opportunity to be able to go on a vacation, but this is why it is very important that we all plan these things together. This is very important training that is required to be at a station that houses a truck unit. Everyone in the station needs to be trained in the event we are placed on the unit. I want you to respect the fact that training like this is important to our family because it gives me a better awareness and knowledge of rescue incidents. If I had taken the paramedic test, I would be unavailable as well. Please understand that these are sacrifices that we are making as a first responder family, and I appreciate all of your support and prayers. Please let us pray on this.

PRAY FOR ME

I'm tired of being what I am not and faking it to get by every day. I want you to know me. My strengths and my weaknesses. I have struggled to find myself. I am just coming to accept that I am different. No matter how much I try to fit in, it just does not work. As long as the Holy Spirit is ahead of me, I'm good with that. I am who God has made me. I'm not a big talker but will speak when he leads me. I'm not a tough guy but will battle if he needs me. I like strawberry Twizzlers and pineapple soda. Early in the morning, a medium hot black coffee from Dunkin Doughnuts. I'm just me. I love God, I love my wife, I love my kids.

Fighting with yourself can leave you drained, and throughout the years liquor helped me to manage this constant battle. Now sober, I struggle because I was dependent on alcohol for so long. I had to relearn how to function in areas that being drunk would help me move on cruise control. This is where I have struggled in my faith. I don't know who I am supposed to be. I know God is calling me, but I know I have some house cleaning to do on my own first. I don't want to hide things from you or feel as if I have to hold so much back. I don't like feeling like the whole world is against me. This is not true.

Pray for me, there are so many days I feel like I am on the fence, getting ready to take a serious moonwalk. I still struggle, and I know the devil wants to tempt me.

My life with you has been filled with my insecurities, and I take the blame for it. I get frustrated because I am not in the space that I want to be. I've sacrificed allot, but I did it with the wrong motives. I still hold grudges, and I pray that the Holy Spirit releases them right now in the mighty name of Jesus. God wants me to do his work, and I have no time to be held down by my sin or self-condemnation. We can see it, and yet we still hope for it, but hope that is seen is not hope at all.

It hurts that you all went on vacation without me. I feel like the monster, the guy everyone is happy to get away from. I don't want to be good on the outside but rotten in the heart. I need Jesus.

Lord, cleanse me right now in the mighty name of Jesus. It's me. God has shown me that I have failed because I was trying to do it all instead of letting him be God. I'm hurt, I'm bitter, I'm resentful, I'm a hypocrite, I'm a liar, but I'm a child of God, and I pray that the Lord intervenes. I took a loss on Florida, but my God is in control at this point. I'm sorry.

Love,
ABC

GONE

My early years in the fire service were rough. Trying to learn a new job and new family at the same time was a challenge. The family was struggling and yearning for my attention. My tunnel vision would not allow me to see what was happening all around me. Selfish ambition at times consumed me, resulting in me not being the best dad or husband I could be. One Spring Day things hit a breaking point. Crystal was taking the kids to a baseball game that I opted out of because I had homework to do. Instead of doing my homework, I hung out with my friend Charles, missing my son's baseball game. Crystal was clearly upset and expressed her frustrations while I was out getting some dinner for the family. By the time I got home, she was gone.

CLEAN YOUR ROOM

All of us have to face judgment on our own. But what I have noticed in life is, when you face trials, not many people are around. We have to love people for who they are and not just set our expectations for them. I have been hurt many times because I did not formally communicate my expectations.

Accountability is key, but this is a word I did not pick up on until I attended the fire academy. Whatever we do in life, good or bad, we must take ownership. Many times people will continue to play the victim and constantly blame someone or something for their own failings. The truth is we need to purge this mindset and take courage in obedience to God.

I know that people have done some wrong things to me, but I have come to the realization that I have played an active role in my own destruction. We allow certain people in our lives, we give in to the temptations, we give into anger, and so the list goes on. When talking to family and friends, it always feels so much better if we play the role of the one who has been hurt. We need to wake up and pay attention when God is tugging on us. We constantly pray and ask for direction while we ignore the signs from God.

I've had the opportunity to go through many changes in my life. The biggest revelation I have discovered is that I do not know God. I've been fooling myself this whole time and following a script that I have learned. The Bible states that when you are one with Christ, all things become new. This means your mindset and thinking must shift.

I proclaimed with my lips put did not surrender in my heart. When faith gets tested through tough times, you truly see where you stand. You can never lie to God. Here I am, feeding the homeless and witnessing, but I carried so much filth and rage on the inside of my heart. God will not do it for you until you ask him. The reason many of us do not ask God is because we are proud and deny that there is a problem.

I'm sharing this because I had to find out the hard way. I had to have certain things in my life removed, such as my wife and kids, to realize I was making them my idols. I put them before God and as soon as they left, I lost my faith and did not have the urge to pray—my spirit was broken. The enemy has used all of the losses in my life to dismantle God's plan for me.

I have used people my entire life to fill voids of my discrepancies. God wants to be our all in all. It doesn't matter who comes and goes in our lives or what event may happen; we know that he is always present. When we break down to our flesh, we show that our faith was suspect from the beginning.

So where do we go from here? It starts with each of us cleaning up our room. We strive so hard to make sure that the rest of the house is presentable for our guests that we overlook the clutter as soon as we step out of our bed.

We need to pick up that dirty laundry from the floor before we start pointing out everyone else's. Sort, and put things in their proper places.

Then we need to get under our bed, because that's where we like to hide all our mess that continues to keep us restless through the night.

Next, we must clean out our closets—there is so much we hold on to that it allows no space for the new to come in.

Dust off your dresser. These are the beautiful gifts we have been given, but we can't see them because they are filled with so much dirt.

It's time to clean off that mirror, take a true look at ourselves, make an honest assessment, and set some realistic goals.

Last, we need to sweep the floor. Sweep all those things that keep tripping us up in life, that glass just waiting to get stuck in the bottom of our foot. Or that furniture that needs to be rearranged to open up so much room in our lives.

Clean your room.

What I have discovered is that God wants our full attention and obedience to him. We get so caught up in all the distractions that we forget to give God the praise he deserves.

Today I got a text message that my lights were cut off in the house. It was not for a lack of money but for a lack of not paying attention to my home. But I am in a dark house, and all distractions have been eliminated. There is no phone ringing, no Wi-Fi, no kids crying, no complaining, no distractions. What is God telling me in the midst of this darkness? He is telling me that *this* is the undivided attention I need to be giving him every day. He wants us to use our gifts so that we may bless others.

Utilizing our gifts starts with a purpose. We have to ask God what his purpose is for our lives and how we can use what he has given us to accomplish that mission. Once we realize our purpose, we must have a vision. Vision is what continues to motivate us when we fall off of track. To God be the glory for the vision, because there are so many times when we just forget what and why we are fighting.

When our vision is established and in focus, next we have to follow through. A big part of follow-through is being led by the Holy Spirit and having that open communication with God through prayer. Everything we do for his kingdom is his will, not our own. God uses us in these very moments to bless and be blessed.

PRAYER

Heavenly Father, I pray for a covering and protection. Lord, there is so much that we must learn the hard way, but we thank you, Lord, for never turning your back on us, for continuing to be the sun after the rain. Lord, you know all that we have been through; you know the trials that we have endured. Lord, we thank you for them all because it was your will for us.

Lord, we are your sheep, and we pray that you lead us upon righteous paths. Father, we have been disobedient, and we ask that you forgive us for our sins and ignorance. Lord, forgive us for our culture that distracts us away from what is most important in our lives. Lord, you are everlasting, and you deserve all of the praise. Help us this day as we surrender our lives to you Lord. We accept Jesus Christ as our personal Lord and Savior. We know that he has died for the very sin that we have been convicted for, but we turn it over to you, Lord, for you are our judge and jury. We praise your Holy name. In the name of Jesus we pray, amen.

CLARION CALL

We don't realize that 1000 years is only a day to God, in other words we can go through years of trials and tribulation only to be prepared for one moment. When I left Rhode Island, I was broken and because I sought him he began to meet me where I was at. When Crystal and the boys left it allowed me some alone time with my Heavenly Father. What I did not realize at the time, was that God was preparing me for something greater. If God told me straight up what I would have to go through to be where

I am today, I would have declined. The process hurts but it's all worth it. When God does something new in us, that we and everyone knows was impossible, it allows him to get the glory.

When Crystal and I reunited I knew I could no longer take my family for granted, but most importantly I knew that I had to be obedient to what God was calling me to do. I would have restless nights when God would not allow me to sleep and all I could hear is for me to preach his word. I quickly disqualified myself because I did not sound or look like any of the preachers that I had known. I continued to wrestle with the Lord until I could not fight anymore. One night before I went to bed, I asked God to reveal himself to me. I did not realize what I was asking for because that particular night, the Lord did just that.

As I slept, I could recall driving on a dark road. There was oncoming traffic and no one had their lights on. It was inevitable what would happen next. I was then pulled up to the sky only to see a figure coming towards me with arms wide open and a prism of light all around. Every color that you could think of and some colors we may not know was present. It was the most beautiful site that I had ever seen. The next thing I remember, I am sitting in the back of a small church. The curtains on the windows were like satin and blue. As I looked up at the pulpit, I could see what appeared to be bodies that were wrapped up in cloth, there were several. I felt the fear of God on me and did not want to approach the pulpit. I somehow was led and could see that the pulpit itself was out of place. As I walk and put the pulpit in place, the bodies began to rise.

When I woke, I was screaming and praising the Lord, praising God for what had just taken place. I knew now that God heard me, I knew now that God has always been with me. It was time for me to do my part and answer the call.

On January 28, 2017 with Crystal and my children by my side, I delivered my initial sermon. This took place at the Neabsco Baptist Church under the leadership of Rev. Dr. Joshua Speights Jr. I have been blessed to have such a great body of believers around me who have help to nourish and equip me for the road ahead. I know the battle is not over but at least now I know why we are fighting.

PART TWO

POEMS, PRAYERS, AND PROMISES

REJECTION

After my initial sermon I knew that there was still a long road ahead in God molding me into my purpose. I struggled to find voice and balance. It's important to stay connected to where you come from but not so close that you get swallowed up. As my walk with the Lord became more pronounced, I felt like the family and friends who used to be close, were now distant. People were not sure how to receive me, I was not sure how to receive me. Many remember me being the wild, loud, and outrageous. I move different now, more reserved because I'm afraid to slip back into a place that was destructive for me.

Growing up I struggled with rejection from being picked on in the neighborhood. As a result, when I went to college, I was eager to join a fraternity. I thought that if I found a group of people that would accept me, I would be good. I was willing to do whatever it took to earn my keep. Once accepted, a true brotherhood became an idol for me. I was willing to do whatever it took to prove that I was loyal. Unfortunately, I hurt allot of people along the way through my arrogance and ignorance. I truly apologize. I joined with the wrong intentions, trying to fill a void that only God could fill. I love all of my brothers to this day, that will not change. God has been dealing with me, and because of this, I've had to put down everything in my life that I was putting before him. Although I grieve, I trust him.

WSSU Graduation

WALK IN YOUR BLESSING

Heavenly Father, this day I am asking you to speak to me. Lord, I feel out of sync with you and I need to feel closer to you, Lord. I feel like I am standing still and drifting away all at the same time. Lord, help me to see it through this storm. I need you in every way and every direction. I need your hand upon me, Lord. Your grace and your mercy have brought me thus far. Thank you for all that you have done and continue to do for me, Lord.

Lord God, there have been so many decisions to make recently. Lord I want you to speak to me clearly on what my mission is. I do not know if you want me to leave or stay. Lord, I know that this is a lot to ask of you all at one time, but you are a God who has always loved me, and I thank you in advance. Amen.

DISTRACTED

My distraction is not to be blamed on others; my distraction comes from within. My life is not my own; it is for God and through the eyes of God. I seek the things that he wants for me, not my own desires. My desires are savage and equate to money, power, and fame. The Holy Spirit has different plans. The Holy Spirit tells me that I need to bring the Word of God to these hardheaded people, but he has also made my head just as hard as theirs. Holy Spirit, lead me.

WHEN I FALL

Lord, this morning and this day belongs to you. I know that I have done wrong, and I know that I have sinned. Lord, yesterday is now gone, and I do not want to make the same mistakes that I made yesterday. Lord, I am looking for you to lead me. I am looking for direction from the Holy Spirit this day. I have allowed myself to become discouraged by the enemy. I have fallen victim once again to my selfishness and pride. I cannot seem to get it right, Lord, but it is your guidance and your protection that I need this day.

Lord, I do not want to fail this mission for you. Lord, let me know how I can stay focused so that I am not falling victim to the same traps over and over again. Lord, your Holy Spirit is what I need right now. My house right now is just out of order, and you are the only one who can put things back in place for me. Lord, have mercy on me and give me a reset. I am sorry for giving into my flesh and not coming to you in my time of temptation and grief. Forget me not, O Lord, for I am just a stubborn child that keeps falling down and getting into the same mess over and over again. O Lord, this day is yours, and I will live it for you this day. In the name of Jesus, I pray, amen.

THE CAMP

When the Holy Spirit leads, we must follow. One spring day, as I was preparing to attend morning church service. The day before, I had visited the homeless camp to drop off some groceries and fellowship. To my surprise, there were some new faces in the camp, all welcoming me with loving arms. We sat and talked for a while, and then we closed in our usual prayer. When I came home that night, something was on my heart about one of the older gentlemen who lived in the camp.

He had told me of his interest in going to service but said he was afraid of being judged by fellow members of the church. I prayed that night for God to reveal to me his mission for my life. A few months back, I'd had a dream about praying and bringing the Word of God to a large audience outside. In my dream, there were some ministers in the audience who were upset that I was leading the prayer, but I could not understand why they did not do so.

The next morning, God put it on my heart to go back to the homeless camp and see if the older gentleman or anyone wanted to attend service with me. They replied that they really did not feel comfortable going to church in the condition they were in. I shared my testimony of how I overcame my alcoholism with the help of the Lord and surrendered my life to Jesus Christ. The older gentleman asked me how it was that Christ had such a hold on my life. How could he experience that? I answered, "You must surrender." I pulled my New Testament bible out of my back pocket and read:

> For all have sinned and fall short of the glory of God, and
> all are justified freely by his grace through the redemption
> that came by Jesus Christ.
> Romans 3:23-24

The older gentleman said that he wanted to surrender, but he was afraid to give up control to a God that he could not see. I continued to share scripture with the group, and when we were done, I asked the older gentleman if he was ready to receive Jesus Christ as his personal Lord and Savior. With tears in his eyes and an open heart, he said yes.

We prayed and he accepted the Lord into his heart. I was filled with joy. Glory to God for using me this day as his instrument. I pray that God continues to lead me to help this gentleman strengthen his walk with Christ through a Bible-based church or group. Glory be to God.

CAN WE ALL GET TO HEAVEN?

Can we all get to Heaven, or is it just for those who go to church on Sundays, repent now or cry later, and go back to sinning on Monday? My goal in life is that we all get to heaven, right, wrong or indifferent. You can smile for the world, but only God knows where your heart is sitting. Jesus Christ has given us an opportunity that cannot be compared, and with weapons formed against me, whom or what shall I fear?

No background checks required, enroll today, no fee—if Christ came to save the world, then why do they still judge me (John 3:17)? I'll admit I've been in dark places, and I still wonder how I made it through. God saved me for this very moment, to share these words with you. Take back what was stolen; take it back to your beginning, no wavering faith, no more being a slave to the sinning.

Many deny the existence of God but mention his name at least once a day. Instead of being your judge, I will continue to pray. I pray for the world, for I too was once doomed. A new life has been given, and blessings beyond the moon. Lord, who am I? For I was made in the image of you, and though it hurt to leave you God, I stand once again with you.

So can we all get to Heaven? I affirm that yes, we can. Surrender yourself to Jesus and put your life in God's hands.

INNER SONG

There are times when God will just wake me up in the middle of the night and give me a song. Sometimes even when I am not trying, I begin to rhyme and visualize the words that are being put on the paper. I am an artist, this is what God has gifted me with, He has blessed me with a voice and vision. Because of this, at times I could be a space cadet, sitting in a room but yet still so far away. God gets the glory, he knew me before I was formed in Mommy's womb.

You Know How to Love Me
A Song of Praise

CHORUS
You know how to love me,
and I won't ever be alone. *(repeat three times)*

VERSES
When I lost my mother, I felt so alone;
I lost my mind; I lost my home.
I drifted down a path that only led to the grave.
I lost everything I was, everything I made.

Then one night when I was out my mind,
I reached for the weapon, but it was not by my side.
You came and held me and never left my side;
Lord Jesus, I feel your love here on the inside.

CHORUS
You know how to love me,
and I won't ever be alone. *(Repeat three times)*

CONTINUOUS
Praise, praise, praise …

WHO'S TALKING TO YOU?

The devil almost got a hold of me today, and I was good with accepting the loss, chalking it up as a good fight but coming up short of the win. Someone is always talking to you because you are somebody. When you are a person of status, someone always wants to talk to you. Well, when you are made in the reflection of the Almighty, someone definitely wants to talk to you. Someone is always trying to feed you.

You don't have to eat everything on your plate. Seek wisdom and discernment in what you are being fed: garbage in, garbage out; power in, power out.

> For I am convinced that neither death nor life, neither angels nor demons, neither the present nor the future, nor any powers, neither height nor depth, nor anything else in all creation, will be able to separate us from the love of God that is in Christ Jesus our Lord. (Romans 8:38–39)

Right Here

In loving memory of Marcus Wright

Excuse me, sir, have you seen the man who just left the room?
I tried to speak, but he left too soon.
You couldn't have missed him: he was yea big and this tall.
I tried to catch him, but I was afraid to fall.
I could only imagine what our conversation would be;
I'd tell him about my dreams and what I pray to be.
Oh sir, could you please tell me, which way did he go?
I tried to catch him, but I was just too slow.
I missed another opportunity for our relationship to grow—
words of wisdom that I may never know.

I wonder if I too had walked that very road,
with a heart of great courage and a speech so bold.
Thinking back on yesterday, my days of old,
would I have listened and done what I'd been told?
Maybe, just maybe, if I wait, he might walk by.
If I'm gone when he returns, please tell him I said hi.
I've been waiting awhile now with tears in my eyes;
I should've just held on when he first stopped by.

Please tell those who follow not to make the same mistake,
for wide is the road and narrow is the gate—wait,
could this very moment be my fate?
Another chance to live and get past the hate?
This whole time I've complained and never once have you stopped me;
something inside is telling me, that you just might know me.
I never noticed those marks or those scars on your hands
or how I tried to move past you and you would just stand.
In your eyes I see hope, and now joy fills my mind.
Sir, you never left the room; you've been right here the whole time.

Jesus …

THE POWER OF LOVE

I've started to realize that the only way I'm going to win in this world is if I start listening. God has given us the gift of the Holy Spirit that will direct and lead us down the right paths. For so long my hearing has been corrupted, I have been hurt inside, so I have hurt others. This will be a never-ending carousel if you choose to stay on this ride. The solution is love. Jesus came to demonstrate this love as he walked this earth and sacrificed his life so that you and I could live. One might say, how can love overcome every problem with love? Could this really be the answer? The answer is yes.

As human beings, we feel as though we have the power to prevent or fix any problem that may come our way. What we do not realize is that we are just really good patch workers, good at covering holes only to have them revealed at a later time. Love is the only medicine that truly heals the hurt of an abusive relationship or rough childhood. It is only love that heals the loss of a mother or father, deception or deceit. When we hold grudges, we become the slaves but when we love there is freedom.

As much as we may try to love, the truth is that the world will not always love us back. As a young man I felt broken from inner conflict and from external pressures. Today I see many young men dealing with the same conflicts. We are dealing with broken hearts and broken homes. Our children are seeking direction and security. We have become distracted in our grief. Our system has made it too easy to give up and walk away. My prayer is that our men and women are strengthened and that our homes may be restored. Historically in select communities, it has been easier for a young woman to receive assistance if she is single than if she were married. The home is the foundation. The support the world offers is all superficial. What foundation is your home built on? God we pray that you bring fathers and mothers back together on one accord, back to their children with a bold demonstration of love. In the absence of a father or mother, children struggle to find their identity and solidify their place in this world. We are not perfect but must do our best to break this cycle of brokeness. It is never too late to get involved in our children's life.

PRAYED UP

As a father of four, I have dealt with many challenges and emotional roller coasters in raising my children. For many years I was lost, and I thank God for my wife because she picked up the slack where I just dropped the ball. I've learned that every child is different, and what works for one may not work for the next. Be patient and love them for who they are, not what you want them to be. I have observed that children need the nurturing of a mother and the tough love of a father. Neither is greater than the other; they are both equally important. Making your house a home is key. Children need stability and need to know that they are safe.

Alijah, Albert, and Asaiah, Virginia Beach, VA

Khalil and Albert

As a young parent, I stumbled but had to humble myself and learn from those who have walked before me. There is nothing new under the sun. Trust. We must be the community, the village that loves, but loves enough to keep one another accountable. Thank you to all the grandparents, aunts, uncles, cousins, godparents, and all who have made endless sacrifices to make sure that this rising generation knows they are royalty. Stand up. May God continue to bless you.

Young fathers, fight for your family with prayer and devotion to the Lord. Satan hates the fact that you want to do what is right, so he will attack the mind of the weak and work from within. Hold fast to the direction you were given long ago. If you do not remember, ask God to remind you. It is very simple, because you are winning, Satan will attack. When Satan attacks, there is a good chance you are doing something right according to God's standard. Listen to your children and be there for them emotionally to demonstrate the power of love.

BREAKING THE YOLK

I rebuke the enemy. I'm constantly being attacked, but I know, Lord, that you are in charge. I know that there is nothing you cannot do.

Lord, I'm being attacked from every angle, but I know that you are in charge. What can I do, Lord, but turn everything over to you? I cannot fight back physically, Lord. I know you hear me, Lord, and I am asking that you break all the bondages destroying this family in the mighty name of Jesus. Amen.

Psalm 91 (KJV)

He that dwelleth in the secret place of the most High shall abide under the shadow of the Almighty.

I will say of the Lord, He is my refuge and my fortress: my God; **in him will I** trust.

Surely he shall deliver thee from the snare of the fowler, and from the noisome pestilence.

He shall cover thee with his feathers, and under his wings shalt thou trust: his truth shall be thy shield and buckler.

Thou shalt not be afraid for the terror by night; nor for the arrow that flieth by day;

Nor for the pestilence that walketh in darkness; nor for the destruction that wasteth at noonday.

A thousand shall fall at thy side, and ten thousand at thy right hand; but it shall not come nigh thee.

Only with thine eyes shalt thou behold and see the reward of the wicked.

Because thou hast made the LORD, which is my refuge, even the most High, thy habitation;

There shall no evil befall thee, neither shall any plague come nigh thy dwelling.

For he shall give his angels charge over thee, to keep thee in all thy ways.

They shall bear thee up in their hands, lest thou dash thy foot against a stone.

Thou shalt tread upon the lion and adder: the young lion and the dragon shalt thou trample under feet.

Because he hath set his love upon me, therefore will I deliver him: I will set him on high, because he hath known my name.

He shall call upon me, and I will answer him: I will be with him in trouble; I will deliver him, and honour him.

With long life will I satisfy him, and shew him my salvation.

What you do in the secret place will manifest to the public place.

CLEAR THE WAY

There is no power that one can possess greater than prayer. We underestimate the power of talking directly to our Maker and asking him to intercede on our behalf on issues that we have no power over. I feel like I am in a position right now where I am losing my marriage because I have received the call to the ministry. I feel like this is a point to go backwards into my flesh or to be obedient and begin the assignment that he has set forth before me.

Every day brings senseless arguments about others' opinions and what they have to say. Nine times out of ten we don't even fight about what is going on between us. There is always some sort of outside influence that seems to be that turning point. Lord, I'm just asking you to show me the way. I don't want to lose my wife and kids, but Lord, if it is your will, then I have to trust you.

I don't want to be in a place doing an assignment that the flesh has told me to do. Lord, I need an intervention. The word *Boston* keeps coming up in my spirit, so Lord, I am asking you to help me discern. A lot of times when there is something on my mind, I read the Bible with that state of mind. This can lead to misinterpretation of your Holy Word.

Lord, clear my mind and my thoughts that I may focus on what it is that you have for me. This is a season of war; everything is calm and clear in the moment as far as the eyes can see, but I feel the battle beginning to take place. I ask that you cover me and my family right now in the mighty name of Jesus. Do not allow Satan to use us against one another. All I can do, Lord, is give you the praise, the honor, and the thanks in the mighty name of Jesus.

FOCUS

Stay focused on the assignment at hand no matter what. The enemy knows that you know, and it is his job to stop you from getting there. Look at your whole life up to this point: every time you tried to do the right thing, there was always something standing in your way as an obstacle. Satan knows that you are one step closer to fulfilling your purpose. Focus, look past all the distractions and do not put energy where it is not needed. There will be plenty of times where that energy will have to be exerted in the Spirit.

Look past all the distractions that take away from your destination. Distractions come in all forms: the internet, television, etc. Be wise and pray to the Lord for wisdom and discernment on what is for you. Distractions may come through people. They may or may not know that they are only being used as a pawn to destroy something bigger. Turn the music down, and pay attention to what the Lord is telling you. The Spirit is hungry; feed it. Let the Spirit lead you where your legs cannot go. Faith without works is dead. We must move in the direction God is calling, and the Holy Spirit will clear and lead the way.

LET YOUR HEART

When your physical condition cannot take you any farther, you must allow your heart to take you where your legs cannot go. But if your heart is filthy, you will not get very far, whether you are the single mother who is too proud to admit her mistakes or the boyfriend who so casually walked out on his family. Ask yourself, was that family really yours to begin with, or were you the intruder?

Lord, forgive me for my disrespect and my ignorance.

I am just a man who continues to act like a man in my pride—my pride, oh my pride—for the secrets I hold deep inside. I was told that I must become like a little child to be invited into your gates. Will I still be invited if I continue to hate? Am I the next in line for God's Holy design, or will I give into my flesh and the unholy wine? I love myself, and who else is to blame? If I don't change the inside then things stay the same.

Jesus, hear my cry. I need you to know I may fall, but I will let you take me where my legs can't go.

RESPONSE

God knew exactly what he doing when he made you. You were made for this moment, and he will see you through.

The truth is, the more we worry about the problems of this world, the more Satan tries to use that to keep our mind off track. God has given us a clear vision and a path, but the confusion of our inner thoughts allows us to continue to talk ourselves out of blessings. We must turn our pain and our burdens over to the one who has already accepted it all for us, Jesus the Christ. We keep taking back what was already nailed to the cross.

Stay focused, my brother; stay focused, my sister. God is near. I know it's easier said than done—it's so hard to stay focused in a world that is just so full of distractions.

Lord, keep us focused. By your will, we will be focused in the name of Jesus.

Scriptures for encouragement:

> 1 Samuel 12:16
> Luke 18:27
> Numbers 23:19
> Romans 8:31

LET YOUR LIGHT SHINE

My gift is not to be kept inside, but to share with you—yes, you. My whole life I could not explain this burst of energy inside that wanted to erupt. And so it was channeled in all the wrong places and was ineffective. I was the child who would get suspended on the first day of school. My mother would be at work nervous because she feared getting a call from my elementary school principal, Sister Pauline, God rest her soul. This would happen too often. What I learned was that when I was placed in the right positions, in the right places, I won. Most important, my mother loved me unconditionally and prayed for me fervently day and night. I thank God for the blessing that she was in my life. I want to be same for my wife and my children.

What are you going to do with the gift you have been given? How can you avoid the mindless cloud that waste your time? Pray that the Lord continues to give us all the tools we need to be resourceful and productive Kingdom citizens. It's in you, exercise your gift and let your light shine. In the mighty name of Jesus. Amen.

> No one lights a lamp and hides it in a clay jar or puts it under a bed. Instead, they put it on a stand, so that those who come in can see the light.
> Luke 8:16 (NIV)

HEART TO WIN

Albert and Asaiah

My Father is a king, so why should I act like a pauper? My Father designed me to be like him, so what situation can I not walk through? My Father is building an army, and I'm enlisted as his soldier. The storms may come and the ground may quake, but I only get bolder. As I get a little older, with more stumbles or more rumbles, I become wiser as I become more humble.

I seek to be wise because I belong to him. It is not me, but the gift they despise. If they hated and killed you, what plans do they have for me? Cover me with your armor, Father, place me where I was born to be. Your blood runs deep, anoints me and covers my sins. You've built me to last, with a heart to win.

My God is awesome: he can move all mountains, and he has given you the power to do the same. God has given us the authority and the power to do his work while we are here on this earth. There is no mistaking that he has placed us in the arenas to be light in the dark places.

We can see because of the light that God has put on us. We can see because our eyes have adjusted to being in the dark for so long. Power! Because of this power, the enemy has put a bounty on your head, but the blood which covers you from the top of your head to the bottom of your feet protects you. Satan cannot kill what is already dead.

We mortify the flesh daily and are simply moving, breathing, and speaking by the Spirit of God. We lose trust when we stand on sinking sand, when we place our eyes on the waters and not on Jesus hand. Heart to win.

SHELTER OF THE ALMIGHTY

We all have experienced the disappointment of human beings, but we must understand that for this reason a default setting was programmed into our DNA for us to learn forgiveness. For when we forgive, God truly forgives us, and the grip of Satan is released. Our hearts and minds must be open to the blessings and revelation that God wants to pour into us. We prepare our earthly homes, but spiritually we are out of order. We follow the Holy Spirit who leads us into this battle where flesh and blood cannot be seen. I shall dwell in the shelter of the Lord Almighty.

> He that dwelleth in the secret place of the Most High shall abide under the shadow of the almighty. (Psalm 91:1)

I NEED JESUS

Sometimes life gets real, and you have to call things for what they really are. We get down, we get up, we need something to cling onto as we walk throughout this valley. I'm in my world, Lord, but something inside is just not feeling right. My opposition has taken position and is tearing me from the inside out. I need a savior in this dark world, a comforter for these cold nights. Every time I turn on the news, I feel like I'm drowning in someone else's fight.

No one is real; everyone has a motive that goes below the surface. I need a savior because I feel like the enemy is on the inside. Every time I want to move forward, I look down at my feet and I'm moonwalking. Hello me! I need an intimate moment with Jesus right now. The smoke won't do it, the drink won't do it—I need to be filled and high right now on the Holy Spirit. I preach it all day, every day, but I need to feel you right now, Lord.

You have shown me too much and have brought me too far for me to abandon my post. Devil, you are a lie. My God is a giant, the big G—little g's won't contend with my God. My God will come through when all is lost, and I'm holding on to a prayer and must carry my cross. I need Jesus in my life; I need to feel the love of God like I have never experienced it before. God, I need you to bring me back to life, bring me back to the existence that you have purposed me for.

Depression, get lost! You don't belong around here. Satan, get behind me, don't come near. Serpent, get underneath my size 12 Timberland boot. God has given me authority to dominate this atmosphere on his behalf. I'm standing on behalf of the Kingdom of God, Your Honor. I'm standing on the promises of God. Mr. Dope Man, I don't need your drugs. I don't want your vile images. I am a child of the Most High God, and he promised he would never leave nor forsake me. Listen, I need to tell myself, I need to tell my neighbor, that God is real and the love of God even realer. Thank you, Holy Spirit, for operating with force in my life. I love you, Lord. In Jesus mighty name, amen.

I NEED TO SEE YOU
IN THIS STORM

I need to see you in the storm, Father. I give you all the praise right now for allowing your Holy Spirit to anoint your chosen in this battle. We give you the thanks and the glory and honor in Jesus mighty name.

In the middle of our storms, we need to see our Savior. In the middle of our storms, we need to wake up from the slumber and see the goodness and the perfection of the Lord at work. God called Peter onto the water when everything he knew of his human will became dull. Peter knew that what he was being called to do was impossible through the physics of nature. That's where God wants you. God *is* the impossible, and he has granted us that impossible power if we believe. God gives us power and authority to act according to his will. I cannot have my mind right until I understand the mind of God.

The truth about raising a child is that it is never over. There is always work to be done. Father, I believe in you. I believe in all that you do, Lord; take my hand and lead me, and thank you for guiding me.

When I don't know what else to do, I call on you, Jesus, because I am weak in my spirit. When I am weak, it allows you to be strong in my life. Lord, you are shifting the atmosphere. Lord you are demolishing strongholds of resentment, pain, and affliction. You are casting out demons in the mighty and holy name of Jesus.

Lord, we have come for a campout; we have come to spend a while in your secret place. I need you in this room, Father, to eliminate the hate. Heal my auntie; in the name of Jesus, we strike down what Satan wants to do, Lord. Lord, let your will be done right now on earth as it is in Heaven. No sickness in the body, no more debt. Walking, not skating, no tiptoeing, but walking boldly on the streets of gold. Glory and honor to God! Live your life for Jesus, forever and ever, amen.

BLANK STARES

What if you knew there was someone hearing your prayers? Would you lose your doubt and conquer your fears? You've been alone for days now, convinced that no one cares; days have gone by, no breaking the blank stares. But when you swallowed that last pill, he was right there, ingesting all of the poison just to show he cares.

> "Come to me, all you who are weary and burdened, and I will give you rest. Take my yoke upon you and learn from me, for I am gentle and humble in heart, and you will find rest for your souls. For my yoke is easy and my burden is light." (Matthew 11:28–30)

TO MY MOTHER

Auntie Abbie, Mommy, and Ma Annie

No matter how many years go by, the pain of losing a mother does not go away. My today is not yesterday, so I will continue to pray. I have been blessed beyond blessings. I never thought I would be able to achieve, but when I put my trust in Christ, I had no choice but to believe. So here I am still in tears, missing Auntie Bea, Mommy, Ma Jane, Ma Annie, Auntie Abbie and Byngo. No matter how much time passes by, I will not let your memory go. I'm grateful for all those placed by God in my life to love me through and through. It does not go unnoticed, and I want to tell you that I love you.

Dear Mommy,

I never got a chance to thank you for all that you did for me in my life. You took the time to teach me and build me up to where I am today. You gave me my spiritual foundation and taught me the importance of the power of prayer. You allowed your actions always to speak louder than your words, and they did, Mommy.

I was torn up inside when I knew you were in pain, but there was nothing I could do. You showed me that our toughest battles are for us and the Lord to go through. You introduced me to Jesus Christ and played your role in the Kingdom by planting seeds in me that would later manifest.

I still remember the day when you were sick and said to me, "Papi, don't go." I was upset and wanted to leave the house for good. Your eyes showed me the importance of being there for your family no matter what. I took that personally, Mommy, and did my best to look after Khadijah and Tiger.

I struggled and I stumbled, but I turned to the source of my strength, God. It was in my season of depression, in my mourning of your death, that the Lord revealed to me something special. God showed me his love when many became distant or silent. Some even abandoning us. It was just us, Mommy, to stand and defend the honor of your legacy, and with every attempt we failed. Mommy you were a solider and all of us wanted to live up to your standards.

The best move I made was to Virginia. It was tough to leave Deron, Sylvia, Toyin, and Sade; this was an extremely difficult decision because I knew how much Deron looked up to me. He could not go because he needed to be close to the medical team that had been treating his sickle cell anemia over the years. Deron wanted a normal life and did everything in his power to have one. Lord, you had your hand on him.

Starting my own family was a blessing, but the Lord quickly reminded me that I was out of his covenant. We made it right, Mommy—I had to be right with God. I was convicted, and here we are, still here, glory be to God. My wife's name is Crystal and at times she reminds me of you. Since being here in Virginia, I have joined the fire department. Not really sure how you would feel about that? Darryl has obtained his master's degree from Virginia State University, and Khadijah has obtained a bachelor's from Virginia Commonwealth University and a master's from Liberty University. Vera has moved to Richmond, VA and is continuing the legacy started at 226. All by God's grace and his mercy.

Thank you, Mommy. It is important that I tell you this. I love you very much.

Prince is still in California with his beautiful family. He has truly made an impact on many lives through his So Cal Aces basketball program. Daddy and I are growing in our relationship; he misses you dearly. If we could all do things differently, we would, but God! Thank you, Mommy, thank you. You did something very special for me. God used you to touch so many lives, and we can still see it today.

Crystal and I do our best to teach your grandchildren all about you. They call you Nana Sophie. I miss you, Mommy, but I know you are resting. Rest, Mommy, until that glorious day our Heavenly Father calls us all unto him. May the Kingdom of God reign for eternity forever and ever, in Jesus name, amen.

Mommy holding Khadijah Sophie

LEVEL UP

Have I not commanded you? Be strong and courageous.
Do not be afraid; do not be discouraged, for the LORD
your God will be with you wherever you go. (Joshua 1:9)

What if you knew there was someone hearing your prayers, would you still have doubt and conquer all of your fears? You've been alone for days now and have convinced yourself that no one cares. I asked if you were OK but was greeted with blank stares.

Everyone cares about you, and God loves you. Erase the hate for yourself and accept what God has given you to work with. He has given you all of the ingredients, but you are still waiting on the end product. *You* are the product, for you were made in his light and in his reflection. Now take back what is rightfully yours, and seek his direction. Take dominion over the flesh that you battle with every day. It is not until this battle is won that you can move to the next level. Level up, young soldier, level up.

It's time to break the blank stare and get a clue to who you are. When you are coming close to your breaking point, just know that God is close. Call on him, for he is near. You've been down and out, looking for a reason to quit. In your search, direct your attention to Christ, who has come to overwhelm everything that has been overwhelming you. Level up!

In that day, you will no longer ask me anything. Very truly
I tell you, my father will give you anything you ask in my
name. (John 16:23)

In the midst of my trial, Lord, you were there. You held me close and showed me that you cared. Because of your love, I have been redeemed; because of your shelter, I have been healed.

It is in God that I trust. Serving at this point is a must. Your Kingdom shall prevail. God has helped me to understand where I am and where I am going. Father, forgive me; make me whole in Jesus mighty name.

STILL BREATHING

You have spent too much time feeling sorry for yourself and not enough on taking action to move out of your inner slum. Every day that you wake up is a blessing. That blessing is suddenly interrupted with complaints, doubts, and self-imposed failures. You have been given the power in your tongue to move mountains, to tap-dance on the heads of serpents, and you choose to lose. You choose to kill the dream before it can give birth. Choose life!

You've been down, you've lost loved ones in your life, your wife may have left you—its rough but you're still breathing. There are people in this world who have never met their mother or father. There are many people who have never experienced the gift of companionship. This moment would be a good time to apologize to God for all of your ungratefulness and to start thanking him for what he has given you. Your kids may not live with you at the moment, but thank God in advance for restoration. Let your children witness what it looks like to face adversity and allow God to perform miracles. They don't want to *hear* about your faith, they want to *see* it.

You and your spouse may not be getting along. Make a decision to love regardless of the fight that you face. It's worth it. God is always in the mix, even when you don't invite him. The proud will be humbled, and the humbled will be lifted up. Fight through adversity with love, and do not conform to the blueprint of the wicked at heart. The way others may or may not treat you has nothing to do with God's love for you. God is righteous; God is just. Let him fight those battles.

Every ambition of yours that is aligned with God's will, will be fulfilled. Every dream and aspiration will come to pass when we stop crying about what we cannot control. Be content with what you have. Be present with the Lord. Don't get so flustered in the things that are things. God is in control, not you, so let the Spirit lead. You called on the Lord, and he stopped by to help, but you were busy being busy. God is your true boss; he is your advocate, your teacher. How are you calling yourself at work if he did not send you there?

Self-check, self-control, self-reflection … where am I, and what am I doing? God wants more for you in this season, not just the motions. You are not a robot; he has given you free will to make decisions he has preapproved. Everything for the glory of God!

God wants the very best for you, so humble yourself and accept what he is truly calling you to do. Ask for his mind and accept his vision. You don't have to understand; that is why it is his will and not your own. I have living evidence of what exerting my will in my life in my season will do to a man. It creates hurt, pain, children out of wedlock, and broken promises and dreams.

You can't do it on your own. This burden has become too heavy. You need a savior, Jesus, the Christ. He insists that your back won't ache anymore from the load you have been carrying all of these years. His burden is light. "Come all unto me who are heavy laden, and I will give you rest."

Glory be to God, I'm still breathing.

Move Mountains

In loving memory of Deron "Byngo" Drameh Outland

We were supposed to see this life through together to the very end,
not only a brother to many, but also a friend.
So for now, my friend, until we meet again,
I will continue to love you like there was never an end.
And where you cannot, I will go,
and because the cross is before me, I will follow.
At times I wonder, What if we never make it to the other side?
What if everything they ever told us was just a lie?
Was anyone truly listening when my mother died?
When Dre overdosed because he could not stop getting high?
Am I wrong for asking a question like why?
Come a little closer; let me look into your eyes.

RESPONSE
I've moved mountains and raised valleys from beneath your feet.
I've slain your demons and your enemies while you were sound asleep.
How can you deny that I exist?
If I pulled back my hand, how much would you miss?

But my people betrayed me with just a kiss,
the flattery from the lips all in the midst.
But if my people who are called by my name will humble themselves to pray
and turn from their wicked ways without delay,
then I will hear from heaven and I will heal their land.
What you think was by chance was all part of my plan.

I MOVE MOUNTAINS!

Every Man

Every man has the right to be a man,
to make mistakes, to find his plan.
Every man's vision begins great,
but success brings envy, and with envy comes hate.

Slowly the vision blurs through insecurity, arrogance, and pride.
The dream now becomes the nightmare; no longer can he hide.
Every man deserves to be loved but finds it hard to share that very gift;
he denies the precious blessings as the Prince begins to sift.

Every man must adapt and react, but according to his Father's will.
There are times he must go; there are times he must be still.
There are times he will get weary and no longer feel that he can;
this creates a tighter grip in the palm of the enemy's hands.

Suddenly a pause, and a glimpse finally catches his eye.
The armor is now removed, his sword placed by the side.

She lures, tempts, and captivates him with her lustful scent,
a touch of her lips, a stroke of the ego—all lead straight to death.

A toast on high, a cheer, a spark in the cover of the night;
the strength begins to fade, his weapons far from sight.
Inside he asks himself, *Is this moment of pleasure worth everything I own?*
The room is full of laughter, but he is empty and alone.

Suddenly a pause, and with everything he has left, he
stumbles to the door, knowing there is a heart that has been
there through it all. She is the wife of his youth, the wife of
that Spring Day, She sits in a room silent and begins to pray.

Crying inside, she smiles, knowing that not she but only the Father can
make him understand
that he is still standing only because of him, after drifting far from his plan.
He draws her close, looks into her eyes, and sees that she truly forgives;
at that moment he sees God and knows he truly lives.

Tattoos

My tattoos tell the story of the dues I've paid—
my mistakes, they tell a story of the pain I've made,
not just on you, but most importantly, to myself.
Not knowing my wealth, I was a weapon unto myself.

When Mommy prayed, what was within began to manifest;
had to open my mouth and pray to endure the test.
So when their response is to classify me with the rest,
I walk in his favor and know that I am blessed.

God's grace has allowed me show mercy,
for those that are lost, hungry and thirsty.

My tattoos tell a story of the dues that almost tripped me up;
my testimony is to show you how God picked me up.

So this breath that I have I'm, going to use to praise God,
and when life gets hard, I'm going to praise God.
There is nothing that he has said that has not already been done,
and when Satan tries to intimidate you, tell him, we've already won.

WE THE WILLING

We the willing, led by the Spirit of God making the impossible possible, have done nothing on our own for so long that we are capable of moving mountains with the faith of a mustard seed—we, the willing.

In life you have to take an honest assessment of yourself and say, "Today will be my day. Today I will serve God with my whole heart, today." This is what life is all about, knowing that God has received and loves you as you are. You cannot really learn to love yourself until you embrace this agape love.

This embracing love is available through the redemptive blood of Jesus Christ. Christ was slain for our sins so that we can be redeemed and declared free. There is no more bondage, there are no more blood oaths, the idols you bowed down to must and will be destroyed. They do not own you; you are free. Your scars don't own you—they define you. Your tattoos tell a story of how an all-powerful God can step in and redeem you with his blood. All power belongs in his hands. All glory to the Most High God! I can do all things because of him who lives on the inside of me.

God has declared freedom for his children, and Satan cannot rob us of our peace by parading the slideshows of our past. I'm no longer a slave to my past; my past is my past, it's over—in fact, it's the preview for my comeback, a prequel to the end of the evil one. My God does not play games; what he promises will come to pass in the name of Jesus.

I am no longer a slave, because he has set me free, and he whom the son sets free is free indeed—we, the willing.

PROTECT AND COVER

Let dry rice be for palava sauce.
—Annie Andrews

You pray for me, and I'll pray for you.
—Jane Wallace Muhlenburg

Your family needs a covering, and Satan will do his best to disrupt what God has put you in charge of.

Not one of us is perfect. We have all fallen short of the glory of God. But ask yourself, What is truly stopping me from making this work? We must look in the mirror daily and stop blaming everyone except ourselves for our shortfalls and mishaps. There is more to lose than there is to gain. Men, protect your family; cover your wife and your children. The children that God has blessed you with are your children whether they have your last name or not. God put you in their lives for a reason, love them. Pay attention to what God may be teaching you through these relationships.

When we allow someone else's negativity to consume us, it invites bitterness. Bitterness, unforgiveness, and envy are just a short list of the devil's appetite. Feed the Spirit, and starve the flesh. We cannot allow the enemy to continue to use the same strategy to defeat the family. Families must fight to hold fast to the foundation of God's Word. The world has no rules; they can call right wrong and wrong right. We must fight the devil, who comes only to steal, to kill, and to destroy. He does this through the lust of the eyes, the lust of the flesh, and the pride of life. Christ came that we may have life and have it more abundantly.

We must humble ourselves before the throne. Remember, if he could forgive our filthy sin, then why is it so hard to forgive others? Love them, embrace them, pray for them, cover them—this is our duty.

LOVE CUTS

If I told you how much I love you, I just don't think you would believe me.
Your absence from our bed says how much you really need me.
When we took our vows, we knew it would not be easy,
but easy became harder, and harder became greasy.
It's hard to look in your eyes; what was there is now gone.
You're standing right next to me but still feel so far gone.
How could everything so right still somehow go wrong?
Another sad day becomes another sad song.

In a marriage, things can get harder than you expect.
You can't be afraid to love, or you may face regrets.
No one is perfect; at times there may be a threat
to an imperfect, perfect union that was left unchecked.

If you can't love me, just let me be.
Break my chains of affliction, and set me free—
free to fall, fall like there was no love at all.
Surrounded by fear,
I look to my help which comes from above,
and because of his mercy, I choose to love.

I will love you like there is no tomorrow.
I will love you like joy rising up out of pain and sorrow.
I will love you for your past, your present, and your future,
your hand in my hand, breaking the vicious cycle of our culture.

Look in my eyes and read my story:
I'm not here for the fame, I'm not here for the glory.
I was made in his image, and you were made of my rib.
I am here to give you your flowers; I'm here to honor our kids.

I am here to walk boldly in all of the provisions of God.
I will love you through the storm even when times get hard.
When complacency becomes arrogance and you begin to strut,
love will make its incision and leave you cut.

GOD LISTENS

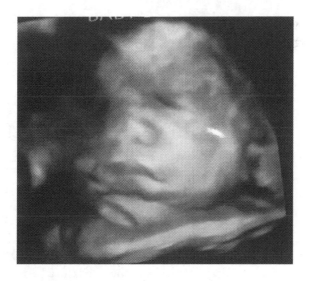

Fair Oaks Hospital, VA: As we walked around the maternity floor that morning, we were anticipating a miracle. Crystal and I were singing and praising as the nurses at the desk or conducting their rounds looked on. That morning, Crystal had begun having contractions. Because we lived such a distance away from the hospital, we did not want to take any chances. When we arrived at the hospital, we were quickly escorted upstairs, only to find out that she was not as dilated as we thought. We were encouraged to walk to improve contractions and give the little guy some prompting to make his way out. Walking the halls of the maternity floor in anticipation of our baby boy coming energized us. We were full of praise, love, hope, and prayer. I never felt so close to Crystal as I did in this moment.

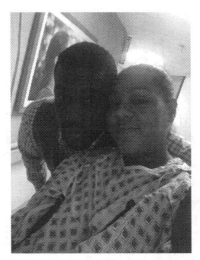

Fair Oaks Hospital, Fairfax, VA

Two years earlier, we were on the same hospital floor when Crystal had to deliver our twenty-week-old baby boy who did not have a fetal heart tone a few days prior. We were devastated and really did not know how we would recover. That particular day we spent time with our son, we cried, and we embraced. We named him Isaiah, which means "God is our salvation." Having to endure through the heartache of multiple miscarriages and losing Isaiah took a toll on Crystal and I. Honestly after seeing how devastated my wife was, I was nervous about trying for another baby. There were many days when Crystal was so sad, no matter what I did to cheer her up, it seemed to be a lost cause. There were many days that I too felt sad and depressed. I felt that as a man, I did not have anyone to talk to. I felt guilty because I did not feel I deserved to be in the same space as my wife.

I still remember holding Isaiah in the hospital and speaking with the Lord. I really did not understand why all of this was going on, but "in all thy ways, seek understanding," and that is exactly what he did. God gave me peace that day, even if I did not understand. I was grateful for those God used in that season to minister into our lives. God always hears us even when we think he is not listening.

Crystal holding Isaiah, August 7, 2018

Fast forward, here we are on January 15, 2020. Today is the day, and I can feel it. Crystal has been carrying our child for more than forty weeks. We have been back and forth to the hospital for the last week. We were sent home the day before because Crystal was not dilated enough. That morning we woke up and went about our normal routine and got all the children off to school. Crystal called me upstairs and said she felt like she was having contractions, almost like a tearing. I quickly grabbed the bag and escorted my wife to the vehicle. We arrived at the hospital, where it was confirmed that it was definitely the day. We were moved to our room, and she was placed on the monitors in anticipation of imminent birth.

Seconds became minutes, and minutes became hours. We sang, we prayed, we prayed some more. The anticipation was building that evening when the doctor came into our room with a look of concern on her face. Crystal had been pushing for more than an hour without much of a result. Crystal was adamant on having a natural birth and our doctor did everything to support that. Unfortunately, it was looking like this was not going to be the case. As we watched the monitor and the personnel coming in and out of the room, we could see that our baby's heart rate was dropping with every push. Because of this, the doctor had to make a critical decision to opt for an emergency caesarean section. This was not what we had planned for, but we knew it would be best for our baby boy.

Immediately Crystal was prepped and moved to the operating room. I was given a white Tyvek jumpsuit, head bonnet, and mask. The day prior, as Crystal and I walked around the halls of the maternity floor, I had observed all the expectant dads in the hallway dressed up in this same uniform. It was almost like we unknowingly were preparing for this very moment. I donned my suit and mask, then I just sat there and waited … and waited.

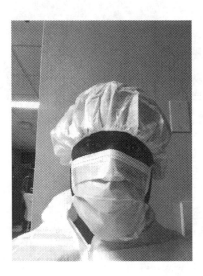

Suddenly a nurse came out of the operating room and said, "Mr. Cassell, right this way." As I entered the room, there was my wife on the table, medicated and waiting for the procedure to begin. I sat right next to the table my wife was lying on, positioned by her head. I held Crystal's hand and offered words of comfort. As the doctor began her first incision, I could hear the monitors and remembered the cold steel of the table that my wife was on. I did my best to offer encouragement during this time shifting my eyes from the monitors and then back to Crystal.

As the procedure continued, I heard the doctor say, "That's a lot of blood." As I held my wife's hand I could feel it slowing becoming cold as her blood pressure began to fall. Our baby boy was quickly taken out, but there was no sound, no crying, no movement. At that point, I was stuck between Crystal and my newborn baby boy. I needed to make sure that they both would be OK.

As I walked over to the table, I could see that they were beginning to suction our baby. Things began moving fast. I was asked to step out of the room as they attempted to stabilize the situation. In that split second, I struggled about leaving, but I did not want to be a distraction to the doctors and nurses who quickly had to go into emergency mode. As I stepped back out in the same hallway, through all the shuffling and organized chaos, I could hear orders given for pints of blood. Crystal was hemorrhaging on that table, and I did not know if my baby boy was breathing.

In that moment I felt helpless. I am supposed to be the provider and the protector of my family, and yet in this moment there I was. All I could do in my weakness was pray to God. I knew that Crystal and I had been through many ups and downs, many pitfalls, but I was not ready to lose her. I did not want to lose my baby boy. I called on God because I knew that he would make a way out of no way. I knew that he was a healer and a protector. I needed Jesus in the middle of this storm, and I was trusting him to come through.

It was in that moment that a nurse stepped out of the OR to tell me that the baby boy was going to be OK and that they were still stabilizing Crystal. I was moved from the hallway to a room where I awaited our baby boy. I waited and waited. Seconds became minutes, and minutes seemed like hours. As I sat alone in that chair, I looked up, and there was a cart being rolled out from the OR. It was baby boy, all swaddled up. I was overcome with joy to see his face, and at the same time sad that I was not sharing this moment with Crystal.

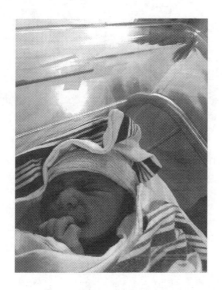

This experience was far from anything we had ever gone through before, but I knew that God was with us. In the midst of all our mistakes, I knew that he was not done with us yet. As our baby boy and I sat in that room, I thought about all of the good qualities that my wife possessed. I thought of that Spring Day on the campus of Brown University. I was grateful for my Queen, I was grateful for good and bad times. The nurses would come out periodically and update me on Crystal's status. They were still stabilizing her.

I waited and waited. As I fought exhaustion and anxiety, I looked up to see a hospital bed being rolled out. It was Crystal. With a deep sigh of relief, I embraced her. I hugged her, I loved her like it was my mission to do so. It was in that very moment that I knew God had listened to my prayer in that hallway. We named our baby boy Azaniah, which means "Yahweh listens."

God is faithful and just to forgive, call on him. The loss of my mother, as devastating as that was, drew me closer to my earthly and heavenly father. I surrender. All my pain, my tears, and my testimony belong to Jesus, Amen.

And we know that all things work together for the good
of them that love God, to them who are called according
to his purpose. (Romans 8:28)

Printed in the United States
by Baker & Taylor Publisher Services